C000298039

The Truth About Grandmas!

Writers

Erika Cornstuble Koff and Paul Seaburn

new seasons®

Kid-tested. Grandma-approved.

Put your hands together for
The Grandmamas and the Grandpapas!

The only thing
Grandma loved more
than bingo was
more bingo.

12

Great-grandma Florella demonstrated her low-tech burglar alarm system.

"We know it's deep. That's why we're standing on our husbands' shoulders."

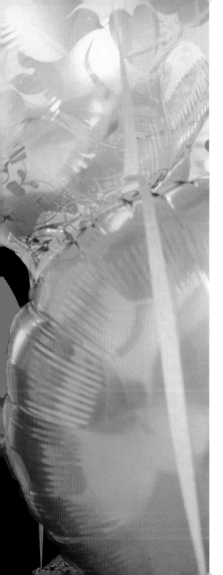

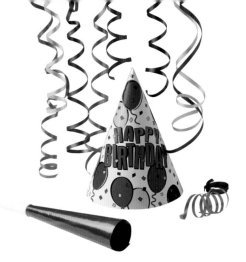

Who cares how
old you are as long
as there's a party?

17

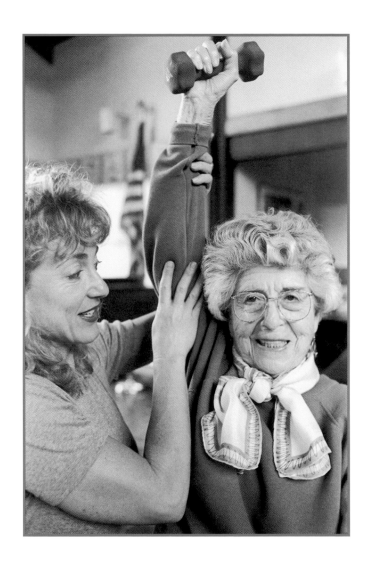

18

With her trip to Vegas nearing, Grandma Rose hit the gym to train her "slot machine arm."

V ictoria isn't
the only one who
has a secret.

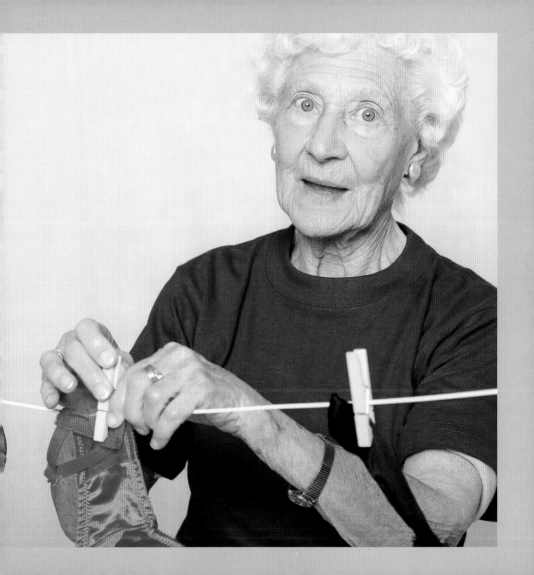

"Of course my clothes are loud—I can't hear them as well as I used to."

23

Grandma beat the telemarketers to the punch by telling them a lively story about the results of using Metamucil.

If Grandma gets her wish, that cake is going to turn into Denzel Washington.

Even if you've read it a hundred times before, there's always someone who's hearing the story for the first time.

30

Decorum is for sissies.

Mildred's secret to younger looking skin? The "linen" setting.

34

"Sometimes I can't tell which wrinkles are mine—and which ones are from being in the water too long."

Doris trained night and day for her great-grandchildren's visit.

Get a kick out of
life. And score a goal
if you can.

It's not about how many candles are on your cake. . . it's about how fabulous you look blowing them out.

41

The best family heirlooms
are the ones you can't buy.

44

"Now THIS is what I call a walker!"

Follow the stars when you dream, but follow a map when you drive.

After years of cutting Grandpa's hair, Grandma knew her way around a cue ball.

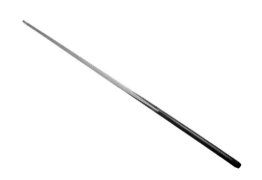

You never outgrow recess.

Even though they weren't related,
Ruth and Esther tried to get the gig
as the Doublemint twins.

Being fabulous is a full time job.

Grandma loves hip-hop,
but we worry about her
hip and her hop.

"I'm not a senior citizen.
I'm a vintage model."

60

If you've got it, flaunt it.
If you don't, hide it in a raft.

That's right—gray is the new brunette.

"You best get your fingers
out of that cookie jar!"

"I know it's good for me,
but it looks like a hat
I once wore."

"Oh dear. Does this mean I put my grandson in the dog carrier?"

"Trust me... When they say 'Stop doing that or your face will freeze'—LISTEN."

Jennie's review of any movie
starring Sean Connery.

"Okay, everyone put your teeth back in or I'm not taking the picture!"

75

"Step away from the crossword puzzle, nice and slow."